Between Silence and Song

Between Silence and Song

SHAILIKA SINHA

Sarvatra
An imprint of Manjul Publishing House

Sarvatra
An imprint of Manjul Publishing House
• 2nd Floor, Usha Preet Complex,
42 Malviya Nagar, Bhopal 462 003 – India
• C-16, Sector 3, Noida, Uttar Pradesh 201301 – India
Website: www.manjulindia.com

This edition first published in 2025

Between Silence and Song

ISBN 978-81-981844-3-6

Illustrations: Shailika Sinha
Cover design: Garima Upreti

Printed and bound in India by Repro India Ltd.

Index

Acknowledgement

This book would not have been possible without the love and support of the people around me. Poetry, for me, has always been a way to make sense of the world, and I feel incredibly lucky to have family and friends who believe in me and my words.

To my parents, who have been my first storytellers and my biggest support. To Vikash, my husband, who never stops encouraging me to follow my dreams. To my sister and brother-in-law, Supriya and Rakesh, for always standing by me. And to the children — Shaivi, Ishika and Veer. I am because they are; so much of what I write is inspired by their wonders.

A special thank you to my friends who played such an important role in bringing this book to life. Deepna, for her patience and sharp eye in editing and proofreading. Garima for designing the cover. Arif Khan, for visualising and designing the book. Raju Kumar Neera for connecting me with the publisher.

To Charul, for believing in me and my art. To Akansha Karan, for pushing me to finally work on this book. To Rakesh, for the amazing photography of my paintings. And to Nitu, for listening to me, for bearing with my endless ideas, and for always being there.

My publisher for making this possible.

And to you, dear reader – thank you. For picking up this book, for reading these poems, and for letting my words become a part of your world. If even one line stays with you, makes you pause, or makes you feel something, then I know this book has done its job.

With gratitude and love,

Poets and poetry don't truly belong to this world. You may see poets every day – talking, walking, blending into daily life, but deep down, they remain outsiders, not quite a part of it all. To a poet's heart, ordinary things – a tree, everyday traffic, a person quietly sitting amidst chaos – take on a deeper meaning.

Then why are poets here? Perhaps, to make the world slightly more bearable, a little stronger, and a bit more sensitive.

The world needs more of them for sure!

All paintings featured in this book are original works by the author, with some pieces drawing inspiration from Pinterest.

Garden of life

Crimson hues paint the Eastern sky,
A little after, the sun awakes.
My garden blooms prepare to greet
The walkers walking down the street.

Soon my garden comes all alive for a new day,
Basking in the yellow sunshine, in fragrance so divine.
Hues of purple, pink, red, blue and green
Dance and sway with the morning breeze.

No two days here are the same,
From dawn to dusk, everyday it's a different game.

Evening arrives with a cuckoo's love song,
And darkness envelopes everything around.
Sparkles of flickering lights, adorn my garden premise
O, these tiny creatures – the fireflies, offer such a
pleasant sight.

Seasons change, the garden colours remain,
Their tints and shades change,
As if to remind me of my life's garden,
Where change is the only constant!

In life's journey for me though,
This garden is the only constant I know!

The Void

This faraway land,
And its sandy shores come alive,
Dancing with the moon so bright.
The waves, like a delicate dream,
Join them too in great delight.

Listen!
There's so much to hear,
This eternal sound of nothingness.
This pure sight bears witness
To all the calmness inside.

Time heals, time conceals.
The void, settled deep within.
It always stays,
It refuses to go away,
And you slowly learn to live with it.

The World Outside My Window

I spot the bulbul and the parakeets,
The dove and the babblers umpteen.
'Tis beautiful sight unfolding right before my eyes,
On the day of April 2020 when I'm stuck inside.

Outside my huge window, stands a huge tree,
the branches of which gets trimmed every January
Out of greed to let the sun shine through.
Oh, how I looked at this tree so differently!

As moments turned to days, and days to months,
within the confines of the four walls,
This tree, touching the sky, a home to so many,
Became a whole new world, outside my window,
the one I love already.

I made friendships a plenty here, that did away
with my Covid fears
My bestie – the Chirpy squirrel, running up and
down with its squeaky tumults
A special connect, that my soul treasured,
When, outside connections lay severed.

Where was I all this while,
Juggling between home and work.
Without a moment to slow down and behold,
A sight like this, ever before.

Year 2020 has taught lessons umpteen
Finding joy in little things,
Living a life in content and peace,
And ways to find bliss within!

The Eternal Duel

If a thousand thoughts have a home,
It is inside the human mind alone.
Ever growing, ever changing, together they stay
While the heart is only an illusion at play.

From action to reaction, perception to emotion,
From endurance to silence, resilience to bliss.
It's sheer brilliance - all that the mind holds.
Use it right, and you'll get everything that the heart desires.

A war between the heart and mind
A battle of winning or making peace.
If you decide to listen to your heart alone, think twice.
Lest you pay a heavy price!

यं

An Inward Journey

And there, I'd left myself far behind,
Such a stranger to me was I.
A hollow, deep within,
That only deepened as time passed by.

You never stopped to find me, to get me back from within
And I kept wondering. Didn't you say you loved me?
By my side, you were there, every day and every night
Like a cold companion, one who couldn't ever see
beyond thee.

Sometimes, occasionally,
On cold winter nights – long and lonely,
Or on scorching summer afternoons with solitude as
company,
That spring which never touched me and the rains that
emptied me every bit.

And one day when I was all alone,
Surrounded in the world of my own thoughts,
When suddenly I heard a clear voice.
Woman, you ought to get back, you have no choice.

I turned back, but no one was seen.
And then I took a step within,
A face I'd not seen in many, many years now.
The one I had forgotten completely, was there with a
grin.

And then I realized that all this while,
I had kept running, running away from my own being.
But why?
That day I changed.
With a promise to be kind to that person within,
And I knew,
I shall never be that me, ever again!

A Selfish Connection

Humans and Earth –
had a connection, divine
where humans held her in high regard
and she blessed them with abundance in return.

The equation has changed,
For greed has made its way.
The giving nature of the Earth remains
Just the same, its abundance has but been
depleted by humans.

How long can the earth support,
This greediness and desire?
A selfless giver every time,
is slowly turning sick and tired.

Now she lies all alone.
No one to care for her.
She's been used to bits and pieces,
No one is there for her.

Humanity is selfish.
It still believes the Earth will soon replenish!

Unapologetically Her

Call me bold, Call me beautiful.
A little playful or even sinful.
I am the woman of today,
A little serene, a little cheerful.

Full of power and potential,
And everything that's essential.
Full of attitude and desires,
With dreams to go up higher.

A creature too bright,
Hearty and full of delight.
I am a bird or a butterfly,
Born to touch the heights of sky.

Splashing the air with colours bright,
With a heart that dances in delight.
All set out to discover,
As the beautiful chaos of life uncovers.

---

*Inspired by Maya Angelou's powerful rebellious words in 'Still I Rise'

Opposites

There's more to life
than you and me.
The perfect opposites
Stuck together, yet free.

Just like after every dark night
Comes the morning bright.
Every gloomy day
Followed by the lovely sunshine.

When there's tears,
laughter comes to care.
The colourful spring sets the heart right
After the frosty winter subsides.

There's silence and it so appeals
Because of noise all around.
There's sensitivity to every extent,
Because insensitivity too is equally present.

The desert and the wildernesses,
the sea and the mountain,
Colours – black and white,
The earth and the sky.

Opposites coexist, often entwined.
This world is just so well aligned!

Pause

Stop and smell the roses.
Stop and listen to the sounds of nature around.
Stop and convey your love to the ones you love.
Stop and let life experience the magic of all the above.

But why do you ask me to stop?
Life's anyway beautiful and at the top.
For empathy, for kindness and resilience, I say
The world needs all of these in abundance.

Take a pause once a while,
Soak up moments that make you smile.
And when life ever throws in darkness.
You'll have all the strength and stillness.

Take a pause,
Right now, right here!
To experience and comprehend.
That's when you'll thank me, my friend.

Little Joys

In vibrant vermillion hues ,
the mighty Gulmohar blooms.
Yes, summer is here, it says
Lining up on either side of the lanes.

Then comes the rain
When promising clouds,
Down they pour
Quenching the thirsty Earth to the core.

The golden Autumn sky
Brings vibrant red, orange and yellow hues
Over meadows and mountains high
Days getting shorter, nights growing longer now.

Those solitary moments by the fireplace,
On freezing cold, long wintry nights ,
Eyes filled with smoky dreams,
The heart trying to evade sleep.

The evenings by the river stream
Daffodils, daisies, tulips and lilacs,
These blooming beauties making a comeback,
After months of wait for Spring.

Nature is a tale of change,
Of seasons, blossoms and blooms setting up a stage,
These are a few of my favourite things,
Entwined together in threads unseen.

Escape

This air, it feels so new.
Is it an alien land,
Or so it feels to me?

Those dark dungeons,
For 10 years in a row
They were my home.

Prison, and not a home, truly
Like a machine,
Where I lived.

Where nights would come alive,
And my world would doze off
At the strike of morning five.

I could never feel
The gentle morning breeze,
Or ever see the rising sun.

My soft cries
and my silent tears
were my only company.

The taste of freedom
So strange, it seems.
Have I really escaped those chains?

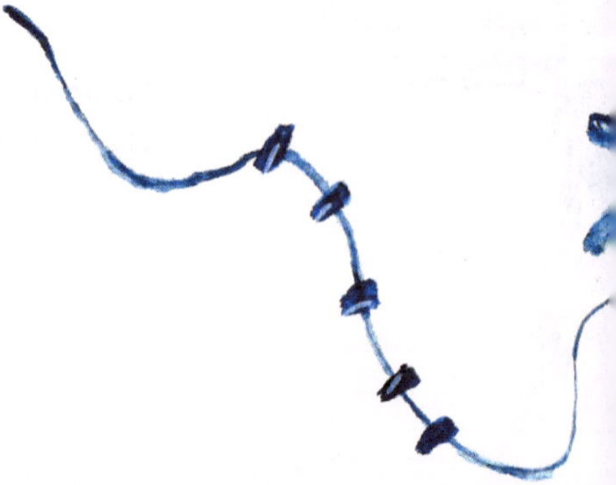

I pinch myself,
A thousand and one times ,
To check if this is true.

This rescue home,
my new abode,
I am so ready to make it my own.

The little girl
who had been picked from a village fair,
10 years ago, on the same day.

Today she dances free
This Pohela Boishakh*
is special indeed.

* Pohela Boishakh is the first day of the Bengali calendar. It announces the commencement of the Bengali New Year.

Fading Footprints

As morning sunrays fell over my face,
I wished to rise from the bed's embrace,
Yet there I lay, trapped within,
With no one by my side.

I opened the door at the bell,
Only to find your footprints bare.
I knew you had come last night again,
But tied tightly to your ego's unyielding chain.

Those feet that were meant to tread together,
Leaving behind a trail of love in every weather.
Now they walk in separation, lost in the distance,
Same love, but wrapped in a difficult silence.

That veil of pride
Enslaves our hearts in no time.
Thousands of promises go by in vain,
Only the footprints remain to slowly fade away.

Being Buddha

In this race called life,
How do we slow down and survive?
This world and its ceaseless clamour,
Where to seek the silent whispers of joy?

The four sights that changed Your mind
Turn around and here you will find, everywhere,
every day.
Just that no one stops to think,
The way You did many, many years before.

We have gotten so used to it,
So deeply drowned in the five evils, without guilt
Lust, wrath, greed, attachment and ego.
Do we ever want to forgo?

To renounce, and embrace a simple life
Is far more than divine.
You went away in search of truth and peace,
And showed us the path where pains cease.

Some acts of kindness, a bit of meditation,
Some contentment, some deep connections.
Being Buddha in the smallest way, it's a long,
slow process
How I wish to experience this metamorphosis!

Possession

Those red roses,
Resting between the pages, silently
Holding on to tales of the bygone days,
Of memories, of moments, once lived together.

The love that seemed so sublime,
With promises to stay together, forever,
Why, then, did it turn away,
Leaving behind longingness and pain.

Ah! those fragile leaves, those tender petals,
Their fragrance has faded, yet beauty remains.
As I turn the pages and touch the red roses, I relive those
moments, those kisses, those promises again.

Why were they all so short-lived,
Those happy moments with doses of little tiffs.
That drifting apart tore my heart into pieces, infinite,
Leaving behind scars for a lifetime.

Time heals everything, they say.
How? Please tell me, I pray.
To them, they are dead flowers.
To me, they are so full of life with memories.

Another bud, somewhere , waiting to bloom,
In redness divine, Not knowing that its destiny lies,
Amid the pages of a lover's book,
With a piece of heart that stays there with it.

A Man I Knew

A man I once knew, so close, so near,
Now a stranger, distant, unclear.
Life has changed in ways untold,
Hearts once close now drift, grown cold.

At the moon-lit sky, we endlessly stared,
With blinking eyes, where dreams coincide,
Counting the stars in the quietness of the night,
Wrapped in the soft cuddles of the mist, oh, what a sight!

Did he get tired of the same old song,
Or did new paths lead him far and strong?
Reasons and answers I give to myself, aplenty,
Life's trials and burdens perhaps made us unsteady

Yet, in this distance, a truth may reside,
Change is the river where lives collide.
I'll cherish the moments we once knew,
With hope that one day our love will renew.

For the man I once knew, though now a stranger,
Will forever remain in the heart's secret chamber.

Change

Change begins
with those
who dare to step beyond comfort,
who think for the society first,
setting themselves aside.

Change comes
through those
who lend their voice to those unheard,
who challenge conventions,
who question the status quo.

Change happens
when people
hold on to hope,
refuse to give up,
and walk the talk.

Change thrives
through those
who strive hard to make our world a better place,
who act with empathy and thoughtfulness,
who become the change they wish to see.

Problems out there are plenty
Racism, Environment, Equality, Education and Poverty.
The list is long and so is the human spirit,
of those who dare to make a change.

On the Other Side of the Mirror

I wish to tell you
Some words of praise
For how far you have come
from where you started
For your efforts
To stand where you are standing today.

I wish to tell you
Some words of praise
For how you've let your thoughts wander without fear,
How you speak your mind without bothering what
others will think
For choosing to stand alone, firm and determined
when all others have abstained from standing by you.

I wish to tell you
Some words of praise
For how you have believed
And how beautifully you have healed
For the will to take the first step
And for not willing to give up.

I have never said this before,
But it's never too late
To say the words of praise.
Yes, I am proud of you
The one I see
on the other side of the mirror!

Eyes

Those beautiful black eyes,
As if touched by the night sky,
How easily, they reveal the feelings
The heart wishes to conceal.

Whether it is love inside
Or pain that the heart hides,
The language of the eyes
says it all and keeps no surprise.

Whether it is worry or disdain,
Fear or complaint,
The lips may be sealed,
But the eyes will show it upright.

The secret lies
in knowing the language of the eyes!

Lost

Flowers dancing in the breeze
Beside the shimmering river.
O what a pleasant sight it is
That makes the heart sing.

Birds chirp in glee
As they fly free,
Up there in the sunshine sky
Chatting with the clouds so shy.

The stony paths
Leading to places unknown
So lost and, yet so own.
Not for a second here I feel alone.

Number

What would this world be
Without these numbers
Whole and Natural, Rational and irrational?

In this vast
Number family,
The strangest one to me is Zero indeed.

From nothing it begins, stretching to infinity,
Both as prefix, and suffix
Or leaves its mark by coming in between.

Zero is a language so complete,
It makes us believe in
the magic of existence in absence.

It brings out the difference
Between 15 and 105,
Just by holding its place tight.

Isn't Zero an amazing entity!

Shackles

Am I a wandering soul,
Who sits quietly by the ocean
Or moves up to the hills
The very next moment.

Am I a kite
That loves to go high?
High up there
Where even sight betrays.

Am I a lone traveller,
Who walks the countryside
Or who sets out to discover,
The land and the sea across the globe.

Am I all of these
Or just a timid soul?
Dwelling inside this body,
Waiting to break through.

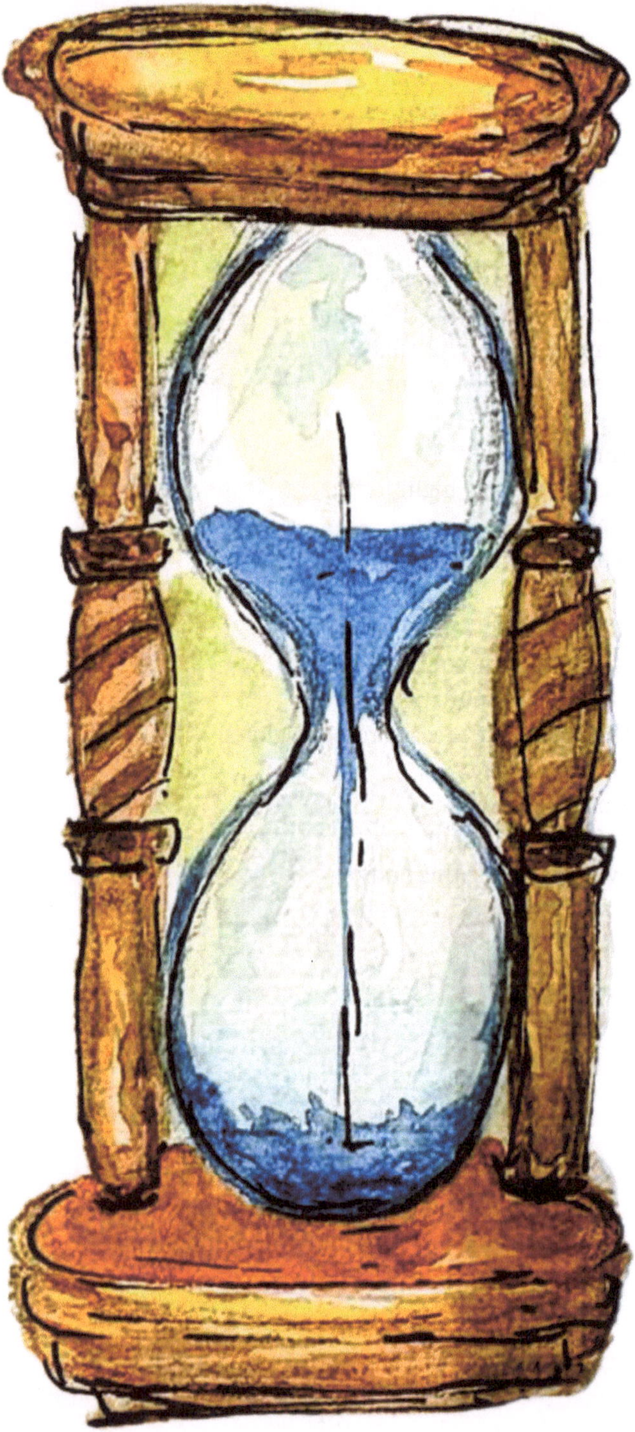

When Everything Stops

Time moves fast
Faster than light
Faster than a train, tiger or trigger
Or even a video going viral within seconds!

No friction force can hold it back,
No objects can obstruct it.
Yet, it forms shadows,
Shadows of the past,
That sometimes linger,
Till the very last!

And then, it leaves behind
A host of golden memories
Smiling back, from bygone days
Even as time slips away

Yet for some
Time comes to a standstill!
Seasons come and go
And people around continue to grow old
Nature turns into a sculptor
And landscapes paint a different picture!

Those eyes still have no pain, no happiness either
Their living soul, with death, is entwined
Wishing for time to move faster, faster than ever
Waiting, waiting, waiting
For the TIME to come!

Weightless

My mind wandered up
slowly to the clouds, My feet
gently left the ground

Whispering Night

Under velvet skies,
wildflowers breathe,
whispering secrets
only stars perceive.

Magic blooms gently,
each petal aglow –
my heart holds forever
what the night lets flow.

Standing by the Sea

The shadows of the blues and greens
The memories of the ocean breeze
Soft whispers of the rolling tide,
Carry dreams far deep inside.

Sunlight dances on gentle waves,
Golden hues in hidden caves;
Salted air upon my skin,
Awakening senses deep within.

It lifts me up, high and free,
Above the shore, beyond the sea,
My heart sails where seabirds fly
Endless joy no gold can buy.

From Darkness to Light

In the darkness of the night
When shadows leave the side
This shining bright light of mine
Leads me and keeps me all fine.

When times are hard
It shows me the path
It's okay, it says to me and my soul
I'll light your way till the last goal.

You are not alone in your struggle
These times are only a bubble
This fear within you will subside
Just take the world in your stride.

These words are a treasure
They keep me going without fear
Today I am free from what I used to be
And this feels so right to me.

Gratitude

There are two choices for us to make –
A life full of blame and complain
Or to be grateful
for every little that we gain.

Love, care, healing and hope –
How often do we think about
these intangible 'little' things
We do lose count of our blessings.

The love that turns our world around
The care that helps us rebound
That touch that heals us to the core
That ray of hope that gives courage and more.

How often do we stop to thank
The sun, the moon, and mighty blue sky
Our loved ones whose kindness fills our cup,
And blessings from the Almighty above.

Forgiveness, acceptance and abundance
Bring happiness and resilience immense
Embrace these, not in pretence
Practice gratitude in every sense.

Not Everything is Beautiful, My Child!

My little one,
with eyes full of love and joy,
It's you who makes me feel alive
After a busy, tiring day.

You are still too young,
to understand the world around you –
Its nuances and its appeal;
It's not an easy world indeed!

Not all paths are smooth, my child,
Yet, you can still walk all along.
Not all choices are right, my child,
You can still choose wisely, I feel.

Not all skies are clear and blue,
You can still wait for the rainbow after rainy days,
Or see the silver lining
Even in the darkest clouds.

Not all voices speak the truth, my child,
Yet, you must always seek your own,
Because truth gives you the strength
And guides your heart to every length.

Not all dreams come easily, my child,
But you can chase them with courage,
And never lose heart
Even if they stay beyond reach.

Not all hands reach out to hold you, my child,
But you can always choose to hold others gently.
Or when words are not pleasant enough
You can choose yours with care, to heal and never hurt.

Not all hearts feel alike
Most won't, my child
But you can have empathy
And open doors and hearts alike.

For not everything is beautiful, my child—
But you,
You can always choose love,
And create your own beauty!

Don't Go Away, My Love

If you were to go away ever
My world would crumble down, in great measure.
Don't turn away, I plead
You are the breath I need.

You make my small, little world
Feel complete
A world that's ours alone
where I am you and you are me.

You are the reason
I see goodness around
You take my pain away
Each time I breakdown.

O Love, don't go away.
In this harsh world,
I'll be alone –
left to stay.

By the Ganga

The golden rays of the morning sun,
Touch the waters of the shimmering river –
Ah, what a sight to behold!

A quiet morning whispers in,
No one knows
What it holds within!

The temple bells,
From far somewhere,
Break the silence in rhythmic air.

A priest prepares his worship space,
A child runs past with sunlit face,
As Banaras wakes and gently shakes.

The tea stall opens,
And warmth it serves,
The morning comes with joys umpteen

Some run in a quick pace
Some keep it slow
The morning is, to each, their own

As I sit upon its shore and watch the morning unfold,
In that stillness, I realise –
A day begins with hope untold.